5
INGREDIENT
COOKBOOK

Timesaving Recipes
For Great-Tasting Food
You Can Fix With
Only 5 Ingredients.

Bonnie Scott

BONNIE SCOTT

CONTENTS

5 Ingredient Cookbook

With just five simple ingredients, you can have dinner, a snack or a meal on the table in no time flat. You don't need a huge pantry with shelves of ingredients to serve your family everything from super easy snacks and appetizers to scrumptious salads, suppers and delectable desserts.

With a minimum of ingredients, a few basic cooking techniques and great recipes that let the natural tastes of good food shine through, you're set to satisfy your family and guests with 140 delicious recipes that will become favorite go-to solutions for every occasion.

Not only will you appreciate these simple, time-saving recipes for the number of ingredients, you're sure to be grateful for how quickly you're out of the kitchen once the preparation is complete. Cleanup is a snap, as many of these recipes are of the one bowl, one spoon and one pan variety.

Fast, Fast, Fast!

How would you like to be able to come home and have a fresh, hot and savory meal on the table in 30 minutes? It's easy to pull off dinner in a half hour when you use recipes that don't require a lot of preparation.

Using your microwave, prepare the Seventeen-Minute Supper. While your main dish is cooking, use your oven to broil Cheesy Garlic Bread while you preparing noodles or rice on the stove. Whip up a quick batch of Blue Cheese Salad Dressing to serve on packaged mixed greens.

You've put together a tasty meal in 30 minutes and now it's time to relax with the family.

Simplicity and Planning

Not every recipe in the 5 Ingredient Cookbook can be ready-to-eat in 30 minutes, but you certainly won't spend a lot of time preparing your meals. If time is in short supply, preplan your day's menu.

Prepare ingredients like chopped onions, peppers and celery in the morning before leaving for work. Fry and crumble bacon to have on hand for several days' worth of meals and snacks.

You can even chop up batches of often-used fresh vegetables like celery and onion, package them in 1/2-cup servings in resealable snack bags and freeze. Then, you're ready anytime you need these ingredients for frying, baking or soups and stews.

Refrigerated desserts and salads only take a few minutes to throw together in the morning. Refrigerate for the day and they're ready to serve when you get home in the evening.

Many of these breakfast recipes can be assembled the night before and refrigerated. Then in the morning, just pop it in the oven and you have a hearty breakfast without the hassle.

Please note:

In this 5 ingredient recipe
collection, the ingredients
water, salt and pepper
are not counted
when calculating the number
of ingredients in
each recipe.

Snacks

Appetizers

Beverages

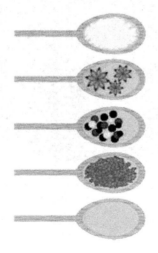

Spicy Nuts

2 tablespoons margarine, melted

1/2 teaspoon ground cumin

1/4 teaspoon ground red pepper

1/4 teaspoon garlic powder

1 (12 oz.) can mixed nuts

Preheat oven to 375 degrees F.

In a small bowl, combine margarine, cumin, red pepper and garlic powder. Pour spice mixture over nuts; stir until well coated. Spoon into a 13x9x2-inch baking dish. Bake at 375 degrees F for 7 to 10 minutes, stirring after 4 to 5 minutes.

Yield: 2 1/2 cups.

Frosty Cappuccino

2 cups vanilla fat-free ice cream, softened

3 cups chilled strong brewed coffee, divided

2 tablespoons sugar

1 teaspoon unsweetened cocoa

1 teaspoon ground cinnamon

Combine ice cream, 1 cup coffee, and sugar in a blender. Process just until smooth. Stir in remaining 2 cups coffee. Serve over crushed ice in chilled glasses or mugs. Sprinkle evenly with cocoa and cinnamon. Serve immediately.

Yield: 4 (1 1/4-cup) servings.

Quick Barbecued Chicken Wings

2 lbs. chicken drummettes

1/2 cup chili sauce

1 tablespoon honey

1 tablespoon soy sauce

1/2 teaspoon dry mustard

Place drummettes in 10-inch nonstick skillet. Combine chili sauce, honey, soy sauce and dry mustard; spoon over drummettes. Heat to boiling; reduce heat. Cover and cook over medium-low heat 20 to 25 minutes, stirring occasionally, until chicken is done.

Yield: 6 servings.

Potato Skins

5 potatoes, baked

5 tablespoons butter, melted

1 cup Cheddar cheese, grated

5 strips cooked bacon, crumbled

Sour cream

Cut the cooled, baked potatoes in halves and scoop out the center. Be sure to leave enough potato flesh inside skins to keep skins from tearing. Paint skins with melted butter; sprinkle with shredded cheese and crumbled, crisp bacon. Place on baking sheet and put under the broiler just long enough to become hot and bubbly. Serve with sour cream.

Yield: 5 servings.

Pizza Dip

1 (8 oz.) package cream cheese, softened

1 teaspoon Italian seasoning

1/8 teaspoon garlic powder

2 cups mozzarella cheese

1/2 cup pizza sauce

Preheat oven to 350 degrees F.

In a medium bowl, with a mixer, beat cream cheese, Italian seasoning and garlic powder until well blended. Spread on bottom of a 9-inch pie plate. Top with 1 cup mozzarella cheese, then pizza sauce and then rest of the mozzarella cheese. Bake at 350 degrees F for 15 to 20 minutes until cheese is melted. Serve with tortilla chips.

Cheese Chili Loaf

2 (4 oz.) cans green chilies, diced

1 lb. cheddar cheese, grated

2 cups Bisquick baking mix

3 cups milk

4 eggs, beaten

1 teaspoon salt

Preheat oven to 350 degrees F.

Spray a 13x9x2-inch baking dish with non-stick cooking spray. Layer chilies and cheese in dish. Beat Bisquick, milk, eggs and salt together until smooth and pour over chilies and cheese. Bake at 350 degrees F for about 35 minutes. Cut into small squares.

Yield: 10 servings.

Cheese Sausage Balls

3 cups Bisquick

1 lb. sausage, softened

1 (8 oz.) pkg. Cheddar cheese, grated

Preheat oven to 350 degrees F.

Combine all ingredients in a large bowl. Roll into 1-inch balls and place on baking sheets. Bake at 350 degrees F for 15 minutes. Serve warm or cold.

Asparagus Dip

1 (15 oz.) can asparagus, mostly drained

1 tablespoon minced dry onion

3 tablespoons Hidden Valley dressing mix

Put in blender; blend well. Use as dip for celery, carrots, cucumbers, cauliflower, etc.

Cheese Garlic Roll

2 lb. Velveeta cheese

2 (3 oz.) pkg. cream cheese

1 cup nuts, chopped

Coarsely ground garlic or 1 teaspoon garlic powder

1/2 teaspoon chili powder

Mix Velveeta cheese and cream cheese together in a double boiler until melted. Remove from heat; add nuts and garlic. Roll thin on foil that has been sprinkled with chili powder; make a roll and chill overnight.

Easy Punch

1 (12 oz.) can frozen grape juice

1 (12 oz.) can frozen lemonade

6 (12 oz.) cans water

1 pint 7-Up

Combine all ingredients in a large bowl or 1 gallon container. Chill and serve over ice.

Yield: 8 servings.

Old Fashioned Lemonade

1 cup sugar

1 cup fresh squeezed lemon juice

2 1/2 cups cold water

1 lemon unpeeled, sliced crosswise

Mint leaves

In large 2-quart pitcher, dissolve sugar in lemon juice. Add water; stir well. Serve over ice cubes and garnish with mint leaves and lemon wedges.

Yield: 16 servings.

Fruit Dip

1 (8 oz.) pkg. cream cheese, softened

1/4 teaspoon nutmeg

1/2 teaspoon cinnamon

1 tablespoon lemon juice

2 tablespoons milk

In a medium bowl, stir together all ingredients until smooth. Chill.

Yield: 8 servings.

Breakfast

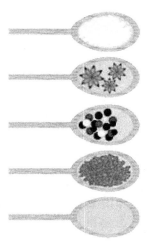

Vegetable Omelet Eggs

1 tablespoon olive oil
1 medium tomato, sliced in medium slices, then cut slices in half
1/4 cup red, yellow and/or green pepper, chopped
6 eggs
1/2 cup cheddar cheese, shredded
1/4 teaspoon salt
1/4 teaspoon pepper
Optional: onion, green or black olives.

Preheat oven to 325 degrees F.

In a large ovenproof skillet, heat olive oil over medium-high heat. In a bowl, whisk the eggs; mix in salt and pepper. Set aside.

Add tomato and peppers to pan (also onions and olives if desired); sauté for 3 minutes or until softened, stirring constantly.

Pour the eggs into the skillet over the vegetables; stir constantly for 3 to 4 minutes until eggs are almost cooked through. Remove pan from heat. Spread egg mixture flat in pan so it covers the bottom.

Sprinkle the eggs with cheese. Bake for 5 minutes at 325 degrees F. Yield: 3 servings.

Applesauce Oatmeal

1 cup skim milk

1/2 cup rolled oats

1/2 cup unsweetened applesauce

1 tablespoon brown sugar

1/8 teaspoon vanilla extract

Heat milk in a heavy saucepan over medium heat until hot. Add rolled oats and cook for five minutes or until thickened, stirring occasionally. Add applesauce, brown sugar and vanilla. Cook for one minute or until hot, stirring occasionally.

Yield: 2 servings.

Quick Quesadillas

6 (6-inch) corn tortillas

3/4 cup (3 oz.) shredded low-fat Monterey Jack cheese

3/4 cup (3 oz.) shredded sharp Cheddar cheese

1 (4 oz.) can chopped green chiles, undrained

1 cup tomato, chopped

Place tortillas on ungreased baking sheets. Combine cheeses, and sprinkle 4 tablespoons on each tortilla; spread green chiles evenly on top. Broil 6 inches from heat for 2 to 3 minutes or until cheese melts. Remove from oven, and top with chopped tomato; fold in half.

Yield: 6 servings.

Trail Ride Eggs

2 tablespoons butter or margarine

4 eggs, lightly beaten

Salt and pepper to taste

1 (4 oz.) can green chiles, sliced

1/2 cup sharp Cheddar cheese, shredded

Melt butter or margarine in skillet. Add eggs and scramble. Be sure eggs remain moist. Add salt and pepper to taste. Gently stir in green chiles; cook just until thoroughly heated. Remove to serving plate and top with shredded cheese.

Yield: 2 servings.

Fiesta Bean and Rice Bake

1 (15 oz.) can pinto beans, rinsed and drained

1 (15 oz.) can Spanish rice

1/2 cup mild or hot picante sauce

1 lb. ground beef, cooked and drained

1 cup shredded cheddar cheese, divided

Preheat oven to 350 degrees F.

Spray a 1 1/2-quart casserole with non-stick cooking spray. Combine beans, rice, picante sauce, beef and half the cheese. Bake, uncovered, at 350 degrees F for 20 to 30 minutes or until heated through. Sprinkle with remaining cheese.

Yield: 4 to 6 servings.

Cinnamon French Toast A La Mode

3 egg whites

1/2 teaspoon vanilla extract

4 slices cinnamon-raisin bread

2/3 cup nonfat fresh or frozen yogurt

1 cup berries

In a wide bowl, mix the egg whites and vanilla extract together. Place bread in mixture and soak well on both sides of bread. Spray a large skillet with non-stick cooking spray. Add bread to skillet, and cook bread on both sides over medium heat about 10 minutes or until done.

Top French toast with yogurt and berries.

Yield: 2 servings.

Breakfast Egg Casserole

9 slices bread

14 eggs

3 cups milk

1 cup diced ham

8 oz. pkg. shredded Cheddar cheese

Preheat oven to 325 degrees F.

Cube bread slices and put into 13x9x2-inch baking dish sprayed with non-stick cooking spray. Mix eggs and milk until well blended. Add ham and pour over bread. Top with cheese and refrigerate overnight. Bake for 1 hour at 325 degrees F.

Optional: Can also add little smokies sausage links, bacon or Canadian bacon.

Yield: 4 servings.

Tex-Mex Egg Burritos

1 lb. ground hot pork sausage

12 large eggs, lightly beaten

1 (4 oz.) can chopped green chiles, drained

8 (8-inch) flour tortillas, warmed

1 cup shredded Cheddar cheese

Brown sausage in a large skillet, stirring until it crumbles; drain. Add eggs and chiles. Cook, without stirring, until mixture starts to set on the bottom. Using a spatula, flip the eggs in large sections. Cook until eggs are thickened and cooked through but still moist; stirring occasionally.

Warm tortillas in microwave for 10 seconds, a few at a time. Spoon egg mixture down the center of each tortilla; top each with cheese. Fold opposite sides of tortilla over filling. Serve with picante sauce.

Yield: 8 servings.

Waffle Perfect

2 1/2 cups rolled oats

3/4 cup cornmeal

3/4 cup whole-wheat flour

1 teaspoon salt

4 1/2 cups hot water

1 tablespoon vanilla

4 dates

Blend oats and dates in blender with part of hot water: add remainder of water with the rest of the ingredients. Batter will be thin. Bake in hot waffle iron 8 to 10 minutes each. Do not peek for at least 8 minutes.

Serving Ideas: Serve with your favorite syrups or fresh fruit.

Yield: 8 servings.

Bread

and

Rolls

Corn Bread with Green Chiles

3 slices bacon, crisply cooked and crumbled

1 (8.5 oz.) package corn muffin mix

1 egg

1/4 cup milk

1 (4 oz.) can diced green chiles, drained

Preheat oven to 400 degrees F.

Spray an 8x8-inch square baking dish with non-stick cooking spray. In a medium bowl, combine all ingredients; mix just until dry ingredients are moistened. Spread in baking dish. Bake at 400 degrees F for 15 to 20 minutes or until golden brown.

Yield: 9 servings.

Cheesy Garlic Bread

1/4 cup butter or margarine

1 garlic clove, minced or 1/4 teaspoon garlic powder

1 teaspoon dried oregano

1 loaf (1 lb.) French bread

1/2 cup shredded sharp cheddar cheese

In a small saucepan, melt butter or margarine; add garlic and oregano. Cut loaf of bread in half lengthwise. Drizzle butter mixture evenly over cut sides of bread. Sprinkle with cheese. Broil for 1 to 2 minutes or until cheese is melted. Slice and serve hot.

Yield: 12 servings.

Butterhorn Rolls

1 cake compressed yeast or 1 envelope yeast

3 eggs, beaten

1/2 cup sugar

2/3 cup margarine, melted

4 cups flour

1/2 teaspoon salt

Dissolve yeast in 1 cup warm water. Add eggs, sugar and margarine to yeast mixture. Stir until well combined, cover and refrigerate overnight.

Four hours before baking, roll out like pie crust. Cut in triangles and roll triangles up from wide part to small. Spray a baking dish with non-stick cooking spray. Place rolls in dish 2 inches apart and cover. Let rise for 4 hours. Bake in preheated oven at 375 degrees F for 12 to 15 minutes.

Spoon Rolls

1 (7 gram) package dry yeast

2 cups warm water (105 degrees to 115 degrees)

3/4 cup butter or margarine

1/4 cup sugar

1 egg

4 cups self-rising flour

Preheat oven to 350 degrees F.

Dissolve yeast in warm water; set aside. In a large bowl, combine butter or margarine, sugar and egg; beat until well blended. Add yeast mixture; mix well. Stir in flour to make a soft dough. Spoon batter into well-greased muffin pans, filling 2/3 full. Bake at 350 degrees F for 25 minutes or until lightly browned.

Yield: 2 dozen.

Main Dishes –

Without Meat

Rotini with Artichoke Hearts

8 oz. rotini, uncooked

1 (14 oz.) can artichoke hearts, drained (reserve 1/4 cup liquid)

2 medium tomatoes, chopped

3 green onions, chopped

1/2 teaspoon dried oregano leaves

Cook rotini as directed on package. Meanwhile, cut artichokes in half. In a large skillet, cook artichokes, reserved artichoke liquid, tomatoes, onions and oregano on medium heat for 7 minutes, stirring frequently, just until hot. Drain rotini; toss with artichoke mixture.

Yield: 4 servings.

Spaghetti with Gorgonzola

1 lb. spaghetti

1/4 lb. Gorgonzola bleu cheese

2 tablespoons butter

2 tablespoons heavy cream

1/2 teaspoon dried sage, crumbled

Salt

White pepper

Cook the spaghetti al dente in a large pot of salted, boiling water. While the pasta is cooking, heat the cheese, butter, cream and sage in a double boiler. Heat slowly, stirring occasionally until sauce has a smooth, soft consistency.

Remove from heat; keep warm. Drain the spaghetti, transfer to a serving bowl and toss with the sauce. Season with white pepper and serve immediately.

Yield: 4 servings.

Chili Relleno Casserole

4 (4 oz.) cans chilies, diced or whole

2 cups sharp Cheddar cheese, grated

4 eggs

2 teaspoons flour

1/2 cup (or more) milk

Preheat oven to 400 degrees F.

Line the bottom of a 13x9x2-inch baking dish with chilies. Spread grated cheese evenly on top of chilies. Combine eggs, flour and milk and spread over cheese. Bake at 400 degrees F for 45 minutes.

Variation: May add mushrooms, salsa or picante sauce on top of mixture about 10 minutes before the dish is finished.

Yield: 2 to 3 servings.

Plum Tomato Pizza

1 (10 oz.) package prepared pizza crust

1 cup shredded mozzarella cheese

1/2 cup fresh basil leaves

4 ripe Italian plum tomatoes, seeded and sliced

1 1/2 teaspoons pepper sauce

1 teaspoon olive oil

Preheat oven to 425 degrees F.

Sprinkle cheese evenly over crust. Add basil and tomatoes. Drizzle with pepper sauce and olive oil. Bake at 425 degrees F on pizza pan or stone for 15 minutes or until crust is golden brown and cheese is melted.

Yield: 4 servings.

Main Dishes – Pork

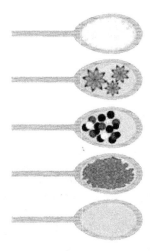

Pepperoni and Mushroom Sauce

8 oz. pasta (uncooked, any kind)

1/4 lb. pepperoni, skin removed and thinly sliced

1/2 lb. fresh mushrooms, thinly sliced

1/2 teaspoon salt

4 to 5 green onions, chopped

1/2 cup heavy cream

Cook and drain pasta as directed on package. While pasta is cooking, spray a large skillet with non-stick cooking spray. Sauté pepperoni in skillet for 3 to 4 minutes. Add mushrooms, salt and onions. Sauté 4 to 5 minutes until mushrooms are done. Add cream and heat through. Pour sauce over hot cooked pasta.

Yield: 3 to 4 servings.

Sausage Potato Bake

2 tablespoons vegetable oil

2 lb. potatoes, peeled and thinly sliced

2 medium onions, chopped

6 oz. cooked sweet or hot Italian sausages, sliced

4 1/2 oz. shredded cheddar cheese

Preheat oven to 350 degrees F.

Spray a 2-quart casserole dish with non-stick cooking spray. In a large nonstick skillet, heat oil; add potatoes and onions. Cook, stirring frequently, every 2 to 3 minutes, until onions are softened. Add sausages; stir to combine. Transfer potato mixture to casserole dish; bake at 350 degrees F for 20 minutes, or until potatoes are tender. Sprinkle with cheddar cheese; bake 10 minutes longer until cheese is melted.

Yield: 6 servings.

Believe it or Not Pork Chops

4 to 8 pork chops

1 cup ketchup

1 cup Coca-Cola

Preheat oven to 375 degrees F.

Brown pork chops in a large skillet. Place in 13x9x2-inch baking dish. Mix ketchup and Coca-Cola together. Pour over pork chops and cover with foil. Bake 45 minutes at 375 degrees F.

Yield: 4 servings.

Main Dishes – Beef

Chili

1 lb. hamburger

1 (14.5 oz.) can chili-ready tomatoes

1 (15 oz.) can tomato sauce

1 (15 oz.) can Ranch Style beans

1 tablespoon chili powder

In a skillet or large pot, cook hamburger and drain. Drain and rinse beans in a colander. To the hamburger, add tomatoes, tomato sauce, beans and chili powder. Add up to a cup of water if you prefer thinner chili. Simmer for 1/2 hour to 1 hour. Serve with grated cheese and chopped onion.

Yield: 4 servings.

Pizza Cups

3/4 lb. ground beef

1/2 cup pizza sauce

1 tablespoon minced onion

3/4 cup shredded mozzarella cheese

1 package refrigerated buttermilk biscuits

Preheat oven to 400 degrees F.

In a large skillet, brown and crumble ground beef. Drain. Add pizza sauce and onion. Press biscuit dough into cupcake tins. Pour meat mixture into cups. Top with cheese. Bake at 400 degrees F for 8 to 10 minutes.

Yield: 10 cups.

Seventeen-Minute Supper

1 lb. ground beef

1 small onion, chopped

1 (10 oz.) package frozen chopped broccoli

1 (10.5 oz.) can cream of mushroom soup

1 (8 oz.) jar processed cheese sauce

Microwave ground beef and onion in glass baking dish for 4 minutes or until cooked through; drain. Thaw broccoli in package in microwave on Defrost for 3 1/2 minutes. Mix ground beef, broccoli, mushroom soup and cheese sauce with 1 soup can water in glass casserole. Microwave on Medium for 8 to 10 minutes, stirring once.

Yield: 4 servings.

Easy Ground Beef and Potato Casserole

1 lb. ground beef

Salt and pepper to taste

1 small onion, sliced

4 medium potatoes, sliced

1 green pepper, sliced

1 (10.5 oz.) can cream of mushroom soup

Preheat oven to 350 degrees F.

In a large skillet, brown ground beef, stirring occasionally; drain. Add salt and pepper. Place in a 1-quart casserole. Layer onion, potatoes and green pepper over ground beef. Top with cream of mushroom soup. Bake covered, at 350 degrees F for 1 hour or until potatoes are tender.

Yield: 4 to 6 servings.

Green Pepper Hotdish

1 lb. hamburger

1/2 medium onion, chopped

1/2 green pepper, chopped

1 (15 oz.) can tomato sauce

1/8 teaspoon Worcestershire sauce

In a large skillet, brown hamburger, onion and green pepper. Drain grease; add tomato sauce and Worcestershire sauce. Cook for 30 minutes over medium heat.

Yield: 4 servings.

Beef Brisket

1 4 to 5 lb. beef brisket

2 tablespoons hickory liquid smoke

2 teaspoons garlic salt

2 teaspoons onion salt

2 teaspoons Worcestershire sauce

Preheat oven to 250 degrees F.

Place brisket in a baking dish. Mix liquid smoke, garlic salt, onion salt and Worcestershire sauce together; pour over brisket. Add a little water in the bottom of the dish. Cover and refrigerate overnight. Bake 6 hours in preheated oven at 250 degrees F, or until tender.

Yield: 4 servings.

Oven-Baked Brisket

2 (10 oz. each) cans beef consommé

1 (4 oz.) bottle of liquid smoke

1 (4 oz.) bottle of soy sauce

Juice of 1 lemon

1 5 to 7-lb. brisket

Preheat oven to 250 degrees F.

Combine consommé, liquid smoke, soy sauce and lemon juice in a shallow baking dish, mixing well. Add brisket. Marinate, covered, in refrigerator for 24 to 48 hours, turning occasionally. Bake at 250 degrees F, covered, for 4 1/2 to 5 hours or until tender. Slice thinly across the grain; serve with pan juices.

Yield: 12 servings.

Taco Squares

1 lb. hamburger

2 (1 oz. each) packages taco seasoning

1 onion

2 cans of Pillsbury crescent rolls

1 cup grated Cheddar cheese

Preheat oven to 350 degrees F.

In a large skillet, brown hamburger, add taco seasoning and onions. Unroll one can of rolls without separating and stretch the rolls on bottom of a 13x9x2-inch baking dish. Add hamburger mix, put cheese on top. Spread other can of croissants on top. Bake at 350 degrees F for 25 to 35 minutes.

Yield: 4 servings.

Quick Stroganoff

1 lb. hamburger

1 medium onion, chopped

Salt and pepper

1 (10.5 oz.) can cream of mushroom soup

1 (10.5 oz.) can cream of chicken soup

1/2 pint sour cream

In a large skillet, brown hamburger and onion, salt and pepper to taste. Add mushroom soup, chicken soup and 1 soup can of water. Simmer for 20 minutes. Add 1/2 pint sour cream and heat through just before serving. Serve over rice or toast.

Yield: 4 servings.

Best Ever Beef Roast

3 to 5 lbs. beef roast

1 (14.5 oz.) can beef broth

1 (10.5 oz.) can French onion soup

1 (0.7 oz.) envelope Italian salad dressing mix

Package of baby carrots

In a medium bowl, combine broth, soup and salad dressing mix. Put roast in slow cooker, add baby carrots around roast and pour mix over them. Cook 8 to 10 hours on low. Serve over noodles or as hot roast beef sandwiches.

Yield: 4 to 6 servings.

Easy Hamburger Casserole

1 lb. hamburger

1 (15 oz.) can Spanish rice

1 (15 oz.) can Ranch Style beans

2 cups tortilla chips, crushed

1/2 cup Cheddar cheese, grated

Preheat oven to 350 degrees F.

In a large skillet, brown hamburger; add rice and beans. Layer with tortilla chips. Bake at 350 degrees F for 20 minutes. Add grated cheese; bake for 5 additional minutes.

Yield: 4 servings.

Spaghetti Casserole

1 cup spaghetti, broken into small pieces

4 cups water

1 teaspoon salt

1 lb. ground beef

3/4 cup grated parmesan cheese

Preheat oven to 325 degrees F.

Heat 4 cups of water in a saucepan. Add salt. When water is boiling, add the spaghetti. Cook until the spaghetti is tender. While the water is heating, fry the hamburger. Add drained spaghetti to meat mixture and mix.

Pour into baking dish sprayed with non-stick cooking spray. Sprinkle a layer of cheese on top. Bake at 325 degrees F for about 20 minutes.

Yield: 3 to 4 servings.

Main Dishes –

Seafood

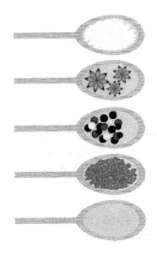

Angel Tilapia

8 oz. fettuccine, uncooked

1/3 cup butter

2 teaspoons fresh rosemary, chopped

4 (4 to 6 oz.) tilapia or white fish fillets

2 tablespoons fresh lemon juice

Cook fettuccine according to package directions. Drain. Return to pan. Add 1 tablespoon butter and 1 teaspoon rosemary; toss to coat. Place fettuccine on serving platter; keep warm.

Meanwhile, in a large nonstick skillet, melt remaining butter until sizzling; add fillets. Cook over medium heat 3 minutes. Turn fillets; sprinkle with remaining rosemary. Continue cooking until fish flakes with a fork (3 to 5 minutes). Place fillets over fettuccine. To pan drippings add lemon juice. Cook over medium heat, stirring constantly, for 1 minute. Spoon sauce over fillets.

Yield: 4 servings.

Dijon Fillets

1 lb. fish fillets

2 tablespoons light mayonnaise

1 tablespoon Dijon mustard

1 teaspoon lemon juice

1/2 teaspoon paprika

Preheat oven to 450 degrees F.

Spray a 13x9x2-inch baking dish with non-stick cooking spray. Place fish in baking dish. Mix mayonnaise, mustard and lemon juice. Spread on fillets. Sprinkle with paprika. Bake at 450 degrees F for 4 to 5 minutes per half-inch thickness of fish, or until fish flakes easily with fork.

Yield: 4 servings.

Fish Fillets Au Gratin

1 lb. fresh or frozen fish fillets, thawed

1 tablespoon lemon juice

1 teaspoon dried parsley flakes

1/2 teaspoon salt

1/2 teaspoon paprika

1/4 teaspoon pepper

1/2 cup shredded American cheese

Preheat oven to 350 degrees F.

Place fish fillets in ungreased 12x8-inch or 8-inch square (2-quart) baking dish; sprinkle with lemon juice, parsley, salt, paprika and pepper. Bake at 350 degrees F for 15 to 20 minutes or until fish flakes easily with fork. Sprinkle cheese over fish. Bake an additional 1 to 2 minutes or until cheese is melted.

Yield: 4 servings.

Macaroni and Tuna Bake

1 (7.25 oz.) box macaroni and cheese

1 (5 oz.) can tuna

1/2 onion, diced

1/2 green bell pepper, diced

1/2 (10 oz.) bag potato chips, crushed

Preheat oven to 325 degrees F.

Prepare macaroni and cheese as directed on package. Sauté onion and pepper. Add tuna, onion and bell pepper to macaroni and cheese. Bake at 325 degrees F for 30 minutes in an 8x8-inch casserole dish. Sprinkle potato chips over top.

Yield: 2 to 4 servings.

Main Dishes –

Turkey

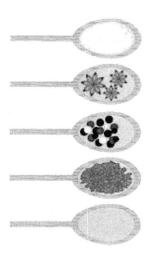

Grilled Italian Turkey Burgers

1 lb. ground turkey

1/4 lb. bulk Italian sausage

1/4 cup tomato paste

2 teaspoons dried basil leaves

4 hamburger buns, split

Mix turkey, sausage, tomato paste and basil leaves together. Shape mixture into 4 patties, each about 3/4 inch thick. Grill 4 to 6 inches from medium coals 14 to 16 minutes, turning once, until no longer pink in center. Serve on buns.

Yield: 4 servings.

Easy Turkey Chili

1 lb. ground turkey

3 tablespoons onion

1 teaspoon salt

1 (15 oz.) can red kidney beans, drained

3 teaspoons chili powder

1 (10.75 oz.) can tomato soup

Cook turkey, onion and salt in 2 quart saucepan over medium heat, stirring occasionally, until turkey is no longer pink, then drain. Add beans, chili powder, tomato soup and one soup can of water. Heat to boiling, stirring frequently.

Yield: 6 servings.

Turkey Casserole

1 lb. white turkey meat, cooked

1 package (8-12 oz.) noodles

1 lb. frozen peas

1 (10.5 oz.) can cream of mushroom soup

Salt to taste

1/2 cup grated cheddar cheese

Thaw peas and simmer in medium saucepan for 5 minutes. Cook noodles until tender; drain. Combine turkey, noodles, peas, salt and mushroom soup. Pour into dish and bake 30 minutes at 350 degrees. Sprinkle cheese over the top and return to oven for 10 minutes.

Yield: 4 servings.

Main Dishes –

Chicken

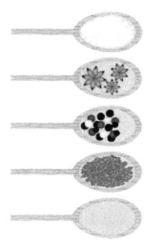

Tortellini Chicken Salad

1 (6 oz.) package blend of frozen broccoli, carrots, water chestnuts and red peppers

1 (9 oz.) package refrigerated cheese tortellini, uncooked

3 cups chicken, cooked and cubed

1 (8 oz.) bottle prepared Italian dressing

Cook vegetables according to package directions until tender-crisp; drain. Cook tortellini according to package directions. Rinse in cold water. Combine vegetables, tortellini, chicken and dressing in large bowl. Toss gently to coat. Refrigerate, covered, until well chilled.

Yield: 6 servings.

Sweet and Sour Baked Chicken

5 lbs. chicken

1 cup Russian dressing

1 (1.5 oz.) package dry onion soup mix

1 (12 oz.) jar apricot jam

1/4 cup water

Preheat oven to 350 degrees F.

In a medium bowl, combine dressing, onion soup mix, jam and water. Spray a 13x9x2-inch baking dish lightly with non-stick cooking spray. Place chicken in baking dish; pour mixture over chicken. Cover and bake at 350 degrees F for 1 hour.

Yield: 4 servings.

Chicken Tahitian

8 chicken breasts, bone-in

1 (20 oz.) can chunk pineapple

1 (12 oz.) can pineapple juice

1/4 cup cornstarch

1 (1.5 oz.) package dry onion soup mix

Preheat oven to 325 degrees F.

Drain pineapple chunks. In a small bowl, add pineapple juice to cornstarch and mix well. In a saucepan, add pineapple, onion soup mix and pineapple juice/cornstarch mixture. Simmer until thickened. Put chicken breasts in a baking dish. Pour sauce over chicken and bake at 325 degrees F for 1 hour.

Yield: 8 servings.

Lemon Chicken

4 to 6 chicken breasts

Flour (to coat)

2 tablespoons margarine, divided

1 tablespoon vegetable oil

1/4 cup chicken broth

2 tablespoons lemon juice

Fillet chicken breasts into 1 1/2-inch pieces; coat with flour. Using a large cast-iron skillet, melt 1 tablespoon of margarine and oil over medium heat. Cook chicken on both sides for 3 to 4 minutes. Remove chicken and season with salt.

Combine chicken broth and lemon juice in the same skillet; cook until pan is deglazed. Add 1 tablespoon margarine. Return chicken to skillet and stir into sauce. Arrange on a plate. Garnish with lemon slices, if desired.

Yield: 4 servings.

Fiesta Chicken

4 chicken breast halves, skinless and boneless

1 (10.5 oz.) can cream of mushroom soup

1 (10.5 oz.) can cream of celery soup or broccoli soup

1/2 (11 oz.) bag nacho flavored tortilla chips, crushed

1 (8 oz.) package of shredded Pepper Jack cheese

Preheat oven to 350 degrees F.

Microwave chicken breasts until done about 12 to 15 minutes on HIGH. Cut into cubes. In a large bowl, combine chicken with soups.

Line the bottom of a 3-quart casserole dish with crushed chips. Pour chicken and soup mixture on top. Add shredded cheese on top. Bake at 350 degrees F for 20 to 30 minutes.

Yield: 4 servings.

Chicken Tetrazzini

2 cups cooked, diced chicken or turkey

1 (10.5 oz.) can cream of chicken soup

1 cup milk

3/4 cup Parmesan cheese

1 lb. cooked spaghetti

Preheat oven to 350 degrees F.

In a large bowl, combine all ingredients. Lightly spray a 13x9x2-inch baking dish with non-stick cooking spray. Pour chicken mixture into dish. Bake at 350 degrees F for 25 to 30 minutes.

Yield: 4 servings.

Crispy Chicken Strips

3/4 lb. chicken breasts, boneless and skinless

1/2 cup seasoned bread crumbs

1/2 cup mashed potato flakes

1 egg, beaten

2 tablespoons olive or vegetable oil

Flatten chicken to 1/2 inch thickness; cut into 1 inch strips. Combine the bread crumbs and potato flakes on a large plate or shallow dish. Dip chicken in egg, then in bread crumb mixture. In a skillet, cook chicken in oil for 4 to 5 minutes or until golden.

Yield: 3 servings.

Hidden Valley Chicken Breasts

2 (1 oz. each) envelopes Ranch salad dressing mix

2 1/2 cups pineapple juice

4 chicken breast halves

2 tablespoons cornstarch

2 tablespoons water

In a large bowl, whisk dressing mix and pineapple juice together. Place chicken breasts in a large resealable plastic food storage bag. Pour 1/2 of the juice mixture in bag and coat chicken well with mixture. Refrigerate for 4 hours or overnight, turning bag occasionally.

Refrigerate remaining juice mixture until needed.

Drain and discard juice in food storage bag. Place chicken on a baking sheet. Bake in preheated oven at 350 degrees F for 45 to 50 minutes. Combine cornstarch, water and remaining juice mixture in saucepan. Heat to thicken. Brush chicken with sauce.

Yield: 4 servings.

Simple Oven Fried Chicken

6 chicken pieces, bone-in

1 cup margarine, melted

1/2 teaspoon salt

1/4 teaspoon pepper

2 cups bread crumbs, finely crushed

2 tablespoons cornstarch

Preheat oven to 350 degrees F.

In a medium bowl, mix the salt, pepper, bread crumbs and cornstarch together thoroughly. Dip each piece of chicken into melted margarine and then into bread crumb mixture. Place the chicken pieces, skin side down, on a shallow baking dish.

Bake at 350 degrees F for 45 minutes. Turn each piece of chicken over, skin side up, and continue to bake for 25 minutes longer, or until chicken is a rich brown and cooked through.

Yield: 4 servings.

Chicken Italiano (Electric Skillet)

2 1/2 to 3 lb. chicken pieces

Salt

2 tablespoons vegetable oil or canola oil

1 (1.5 oz.) package dry spaghetti sauce mix

1 (8 oz.) can tomatoes

Sprinkle salt on chicken. Preheat electric skillet to about 350 degrees F. Add vegetable oil or canola oil; add chicken; brown slowly, 15 to 20 minutes; spoon off fat.

In a medium bowl, mix 1 tablespoon spaghetti-sauce mix (dry) and tomatoes; pour over chicken. Cover; reduce heat to 250 degrees F. Cook until tender, 45 to 60 minutes; turn chicken occasionally.

Yield: 4 servings.

Chicken and Broccoli

1 (10 oz.) pkg. frozen broccoli, cooked

2 cups cooked chicken

1 (10.5 oz.) can cream of chicken soup

3/4 cup grated cheese

Paprika

Preheat oven to 325 degrees F.

Arrange broccoli and chicken in 8x8x2-inch baking dish. Cover with soup. Sprinkle cheese and paprika over top. Bake at 325 degrees for 15 minutes.

Yield: 2 to 3 servings.

Peachy-Keen Chicken Roast

8 to 10 chicken pieces, bone-in

1 (29 oz.) can peach halves in heavy syrup (drain, but reserve syrup)

2 tablespoons soy sauce

1/2 cup butter or margarine

1 teaspoon Accent

Preheat oven to 375 degrees F.

In a large roasting pan, place the pieces of chicken, skin side up. In a saucepan, heat the syrup from the peaches to just below boiling point. Remove from heat and add soy sauce, butter or margarine and Accent. Baste each piece of chicken generously with mixture. Bake at 375 degrees F for 1 1/2 hours, basting frequently.

When the chicken is golden brown and tender enough to pierce with a fork, place the peach halves, hole side up, around the chicken. Return to the oven for an additional 8 minutes or until the peaches are warmed through.

Yield: 4 to 5 servings.

Scalloped Chicken

1 cooked chicken, boneless and skinless

2 cups cracker crumbs

2 eggs, beaten

3 cups chicken broth

Salt and pepper to taste

1/2 cup cream

Preheat oven to 350 degrees F.

Cut chicken into bite-size pieces. In a large bowl, combine chicken, cracker crumbs, eggs, chicken broth and salt and pepper. Spray a 13x9x2-inch baking dish with non-stick cooking spray. Pour chicken mixture in baking dish. Pour cream over top; bake 45 minutes at 350 degrees F.

Yield: 4 servings.

Easy Chicken Parmesan

1 (26 oz.) jar spaghetti sauce

6 tablespoons grated parmesan cheese, divided

6 boneless chicken breast halves

1 1/2 cups shredded mozzarella cheese

Preheat oven to 375 degrees F.

Pour spaghetti sauce into a 13x9x2-inch baking dish. Stir in 1/4 cup of parmesan cheese. Add chicken; turn chicken over, coating both sides with sauce. Cover dish with foil.

Bake 30 minutes uncovered. Top with mozzarella cheese and remaining 2 tablespoons of parmesan cheese; continue baking 5 minutes or until cheese is melted and chicken is cooked through.

Yield: 6 servings.

Sunday Chicken

1 large lemon

1 (3-lb.) broiler-fryer chicken

1 tablespoon olive oil

1 tablespoon dried rosemary

1 tablespoon Creole seasoning

Preheat oven to 400 degrees F.

Cut lemon in half, and squeeze juice over chicken. Put lemon halves in cavity of chicken. Brush oil on chicken, and sprinkle with rosemary and Creole seasoning.

Bake in roasting pan at 400 degrees F for 50 to 60 minutes or until a meat thermometer inserted in thigh registers 180 degrees F, basting occasionally with pan drippings.

Yield: 4 servings.

Cheesy Italian Chicken Bake

2 cups tomato pasta sauce

1 (14 to 16 oz.) package chicken breast tenders, boneless and skinless

1 1/2 cups shredded Italian cheese blend

8 oz. uncooked spaghetti noodles

Preheat oven to 350 degrees F.

Spoon 1 cup of the pasta sauce in a 2-quart baking dish; spread evenly. Top with chicken tenders in single layer. Spoon the remaining 1 cup pasta sauce over chicken. Sprinkle with cheese.

Bake at 350 degrees F uncovered for 30 to 35 minutes or until mixture is bubbly and chicken is no longer pink in center. Meanwhile, cook spaghetti as directed on package; drain. Serve chicken and sauce over spaghetti.

Yield: 4 servings.

Chicken Nuggets

8 skinless, boneless chicken breast halves – cut into small chunks

Vegetable oil

3 cups all-purpose flour

3 tablespoons garlic salt

1 tablespoon ground black pepper

4 eggs

Heat 1 inch oil to 350 degrees F in a large skillet or saucepan. In a bowl, combine flour, garlic salt, and pepper. In another bowl, lightly beat the eggs. Dip the chicken pieces individually into the flour mixture, then into the beaten egg dip, and back into the flour mixture.

Place the coated chicken pieces on a plate until all the chicken has been coated. Cook the chicken in batches in the hot oil until golden brown and no longer pink in the center, about 6 to 7 minutes.

Yield: 8 servings.

Tarragon Chicken

4 chicken breast halves, skinless and boneless

1/4 teaspoon salt

1/4 teaspoon pepper

1/2 cup low-fat sour cream

2 tablespoons honey mustard

1 teaspoon dried tarragon

Coat a nonstick skillet with non-stick cooking spray; place over medium-high heat until hot. Sprinkle chicken with salt and pepper and place in pan; cook 15 minutes or until chicken is done, turning occasionally.

Remove chicken from pan; keep warm. Stir sour cream, honey mustard and tarragon into pan; cook until heated through. Spoon over chicken.

Yield: 4 servings.

Quick Barbecued Chicken 'N' Rice

1 1/2 cups uncooked instant rice

1 cup chicken broth

6 chicken breast halves, boneless and skinless

1 1/4 cups barbecue sauce

1 tablespoon dried minced onion

Preheat oven to 375 degrees F.

In a large bowl, mix together rice and chicken broth. Spray an 11 x 7 x 2" baking dish with non-stick cooking spray. Pour broth mixture into baking dish. Top with chicken breasts.

Combine barbecue sauce and onion; pour over chicken. Bake, uncovered, at 375 degrees F for 25 to 30 minutes or until the rice is tender and meat juices run clear.

Yield: 4 to 6 servings.

Creamy Chicken Bake

6 chicken breasts, cut in half

1 (5 oz.) package dried beef

12 slices bacon

1 (10.5 oz.) can cream of mushroom soup

1 cup sour cream

Preheat oven to 300 degrees F.

Tear dried beef into pieces and sprinkle in bottom of a large casserole dish. Wrap a strip of bacon around each chicken piece and put into a baking dish.

Combine soup and sour cream until well blended. Spread over chicken. Cover with foil; bake at 300 degrees F for 2 hours. Remove foil and bake, uncovered, for 1 hour.

Yield: 12 servings.

Oriental Quick Chicken

1 (10.5 oz.) can chicken a la king

1 (5 oz.) can chicken, diced

1/4 cup light cream

1 to 2 tablespoons candied ginger, chopped

1/4 cup slivered blanched almonds, toasted

In a medium saucepan, combine chicken a la king, chicken, cream and ginger. Simmer uncovered 5 minutes, stirring occasionally. Add toasted almonds. Serve over hot fluffy rice.

Yield: 4 servings.

Soups and

Sandwiches

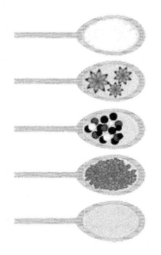

Home-Style Cream of Tomato Soup

2 tablespoons margarine or butter

1/4 cup onion, chopped

1/2 cup mashed potato flakes

2 (16 oz.) cans stewed tomatoes, cut up

3 cups milk

1/4 teaspoon salt

1/8 teaspoon pepper

Melt margarine or butter in a large saucepan over medium heat. Add onion; cook 1 to 2 minutes until onion is crisp-tender. Add potato flakes, tomatoes, milk, salt and pepper; cook uncovered for 8 to 10 minutes or until thoroughly heated, stirring frequently.

Yield: 4 servings.

Southwest Barbecued Chicken Sandwiches

1 1/2 cups shredded cooked chicken

1/2 cup barbecue sauce

1/2 cup chunky salsa

2 tablespoons sliced green onions

5 whole grain buns, split, toasted if desired

In a medium saucepan, combine chicken, barbecue sauce, salsa and green onions; mix well. Cook over low heat for 10 minutes, stirring occasionally. Serve on buns.

Yield: 5 sandwiches.

Potato Onion Soup

6 medium potatoes, peeled and sliced

3 medium onions, finely chopped

5 tablespoons parsley, finely chopped

2 quarts water

1 tablespoon soy flour

1 tablespoon oat flour

Salt to taste

In a large saucepan, simmer potatoes, onions and parsley in water until tender. In a small bowl, mix the soy and oat flour in a little water and gradually add to the hot vegetables stirring constantly. Let the mixture boil another 5 minutes.

Yield: 12 servings.

Salads and

Dressings

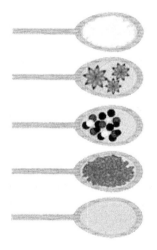

Macaroni Salad

1 (8 oz.) package shell macaroni, cooked

2 medium tomatoes, diced

1 medium cucumber, diced

1 green bell pepper, diced

Miracle Whip

Salt and pepper to taste

Combine macaroni, tomatoes, cucumber and bell pepper. Toss with salt, pepper and Miracle Whip, to taste. Refrigerate overnight.

Yield: 4 servings.

Pistachio Salad

1 (3.4 oz.) box instant pistachio pudding

1 (16 oz.) can crushed pineapple, undrained

1 (22 oz.) carton cottage cheese

1 (12 oz.) carton refrigerated whipped topping

1 package pecan chips

In a large bowl, combine pudding, pineapple and cottage cheese. Blend in whipped topping. Add pecan chips.

Yield: 4 servings.

Instant Salad

1 (24 oz.) carton cottage cheese

1 (3 oz.) package strawberry jello

1 (8 oz.) carton refrigerated whipped topping.

In a large bowl, combine cottage cheese with dry jello; mix well. Stir in whipped topping. Refrigerate for 2 to 3 hours before serving.

Optional: Stir in sliced strawberries.

Yield: 4 servings.

Easy Cherry Salad

1 (20 oz.) can crushed pineapple, with juice

1 (3 oz.) package cherry jello

1 (16 oz.) carton cottage cheese

2 cups refrigerated whipped topping

1/2 teaspoon almond extract

In a saucepan, heat pineapple with juice over medium-high heat. Heat pineapple, fruit and juice. Let come to a boil; remove from heat and add jello. Refrigerate until partially set. Stir in cottage cheese, whipped topping and almond extract; chill until set.

Yield: 4 servings.

Blue Cheese Salad Dressing

1 cup sour cream

3 or 4 tablespoons red wine vinegar

1/4 teaspoon black pepper

1/4 cup olive oil

1/4 teaspoon garlic salt

3 or 5 oz. blue cheese

In a medium bowl, combine all ingredients; whip together until well mixed.

Cherry Pie Filling Salad

1 (21 oz.) can cherry pie filling

1 (30 oz.) can fruit cocktail, drained

1 (16 oz.) carton sour cream

In a large bowl, combine all ingredients and refrigerate at least one hour before serving.

Yield: 4 to 6 servings.

Mandarin Orange Salad

1 (6 oz.) package orange jello

2 cups hot water

1 (12 oz.) can frozen orange juice with water to make 2 cups

2 or 3 (11 oz.) cans mandarin oranges

1 (3 oz.) package cream cheese, grated

In a large bowl, combine jello and hot water. Add orange juice with water. Refrigerate until jello begins to set; then stir in oranges. Add grated cream cheese on top.

Yield: 6 servings.

Frozen Cranberry Salad

3 ripe bananas, mashed

1 (16 oz.) can whole cranberry sauce

1 (8 oz.) carton refrigerated whipped topping

1 (8 oz.) can crushed pineapple, drained

In a large bowl, combine all ingredients. Pour into mold or baking dish and freeze.

Yield: 4 to 6 servings.

Carrot Salad

3 cups carrots, shredded

1/2 cup pecans, chopped

1/2 cup pineapple chunks, unsweetened, drained

1/2 cup dates, chopped

1/8 teaspoon salt

3 tablespoons orange juice

In a large bowl, combine all ingredients and refrigerate.

Yield: 8 servings.

Fruit Salad

1 (29 oz.) cans mandarin oranges

1 (20 oz.) can chunk pineapple

1 (3.4 oz.) box instant vanilla pudding mix

3 or 4 ripe bananas

6 to 8 oz. fresh fruit (cherries, strawberries, etc.)

Drain oranges. In a large bowl, combine pineapple, oranges and pudding mix the night before. Add bananas and fruit right before serving.

Yield: 4 servings.

Italian Spaghetti Salad

1 (7 oz.) package spaghetti, broken into thirds

2 cups frozen mixed vegetables

1/4 cup red onion, chopped

1 medium tomato, chopped

1/2 cup Italian dressing

Cook spaghetti noodles according to package instructions, adding frozen vegetables during last 6 minutes of cooking time; cook until vegetables are tender. Drain; rinse with cold water to cool. Drain well.

In a medium bowl, place the cooled spaghetti and vegetables. Add onion, tomato and Italian dressing; toss to coat. Cover; refrigerate at least 1 hour to blend flavors before serving.

Yield: 8 servings.

Side Dishes

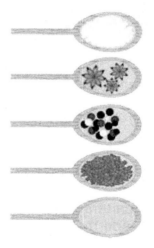

Teriyaki Potatoes

1 1/2 lbs. small red potatoes

1 tablespoon margarine or butter

1 tablespoon soy sauce or teriyaki

1/4 teaspoon Italian seasoning

1/8 teaspoon black pepper

1/8 teaspoon cayenne pepper

Cut potatoes into quarters and place in a 1 1/2-quart microwave-safe dish. Add margarine or butter, soy sauce or teriyaki, Italian seasoning, black pepper and cayenne pepper; toss to coat.

Cover and microwave on high for 13 to 16 minutes, or until potatoes are tender, stirring after each 3 or 4 minutes.

Yield: 6 servings.

Perfect Potatoes

6 medium potatoes

3 cups shredded cheddar cheese

1/4 cup margarine

1 1/2 cups sour cream

1/3 cup chopped green onion tops

1 teaspoon salt

1/4 teaspoon pepper

Preheat oven to 350 degrees F.

In a large saucepan, boil potatoes in skins. Cool and peel. Shred coarsely, using a grater. Combine cheese and margarine in a saucepan over low heat, stirring until melted together.

Remove from heat and blend in sour cream, onion tops, salt and pepper. Fold in potatoes. Turn into greased casserole. Bake 25 minutes at 350 degrees.

Yield: 8 servings.

Twice-Baked Potatoes

4 large baking potatoes

1/3 to 1/2 cup milk

1/4 cup margarine, softened

1/2 teaspoon salt

1/4 teaspoon pepper

1/2 cup shredded American cheese

Preheat oven to 375 degrees F.

Rub 4 large baking potatoes with vegetable oil; prick with fork. Bake on a baking sheet at 375 degrees F until potatoes are tender, 1 to 1 1/4 hours.

Cut slice from top of each potato; scoop out inside leaving a thin shell. Mash potatoes. Add milk in small amounts, beating after each addition. Add margarine, salt and pepper; beat until fluffy. Fill shells with potatoes; sprinkle with shredded cheese. Bake on a baking sheet at 375 degrees F until golden, about 20 minutes.

Yield: 4 servings.

Cheese-Stuffed Potatoes

4 large baking potatoes

2/3 cup low-fat (2%) cottage cheese

1 medium cucumber, pared, seeded and chopped

2 tablespoons chives, chopped

Optional - Chili powder or paprika to garnish

Preheat oven to 425 degrees F.

Wrap potatoes in foil and bake in oven for 1 hour at 425 degrees F or until tender.

Cut potatoes in half lengthwise; scoop out pulp, leaving 1/2" firm shells. Place pulp in medium bowl; mash. Add cottage cheese, cucumber and chives to mashed potato pulp; mix well. Divide potato pulp mixture evenly among potato shells.

Spray a baking sheet with non-stick cooking spray; place potatoes on baking sheet. Sprinkle with chili powder or paprika; bake at 350 degrees F for 10 minutes, until filling is heated.

Yield: 4 servings.

Cream Cheese Mashed Potatoes

9 large potatoes, peeled

1 cup sour cream

2 teaspoons salt

1/4 teaspoon pepper

1 (3 oz.) package cream cheese

2 tablespoons butter

Preheat oven to 350 degrees F.

In a large saucepan, cook peeled potatoes in boiling water. When cooked, drain and mash until smooth. Add sour cream, salt, pepper, cream cheese and butter. Beat until light and fluffy. Place in a greased casserole dish and dot with butter. Bake at 350 degrees F for 30 minutes or until hot.

Yield: 6 to 8 servings.

Creamy Crockpot Potatoes

5 large potatoes, thinly sliced

8 cheddar cheese slices

1 large onion, sliced

4 pork chops or ham slices, cooked and cubed

2 (10.5 oz. each) cans cream of mushroom soup

Layer in crockpot in following order: 1/4 of potatoes, meat, onion, 2 cheese slices (cut in strips). Repeat. Top with 1 can of soup. Repeat layering 2 more times. Add second can of soup on top. Cook on low for 8 to 10 hours.

Yield: 4 servings.

Garlic Mashed Potatoes

1 lb. baking potatoes

1/4 cup light cream cheese with garlic and spices

1/2 cup fat-free milk

1/8 teaspoon salt

1/4 teaspoon pepper

Scrub potatoes, prick several times with a fork. Place on a shallow microwave-safe platter. Cover loosely with wax paper. Microwave on HIGH 6 minutes, turn the potatoes over and microwave 6 more minutes. If the potatoes are not fully cooked, continue to microwave in 1 minute increments.

Mash potatoes slightly with a potato masher. Add cream cheese, milk, salt and pepper; mash to desired consistency.

Yield: 4 servings.

Shoestring Sweet Potatoes

2 large sweet potatoes, cut into very thin strips

2 teaspoons olive oil

1/4 teaspoon salt

1/4 teaspoon pepper

Preheat oven to 450 degrees F.

Place potato strips on a baking sheet coated with cooking spray. Coat potatoes lightly with non-stick cooking spray. Drizzle with oil; sprinkle with salt and pepper. Bake at 450 degrees F for 20 to 25 minutes or until browned.

Yield: 4 servings.

Peanutty Sweet Potatoes

1 (18 oz.) can sweet potatoes

1/2 cup peanut butter

1/2 cup orange juice

1/4 cup brown sugar, packed

1/2 teaspoon salt

1 cup small white marshmallows

Preheat oven to 325 degrees F.

Drain and mash the sweet potatoes. In a large bowl, combine sweet potatoes, peanut butter, orange juice, brown sugar and salt. Pour into a greased 9-inch pie plate.

Bake at 350 degrees F for 20 to 25 minutes. Remove from oven; top with marshmallows. Bake 5 minutes longer or until marshmallows are lightly browned.

Yield: 4 to 6 servings.

Tater Tot Casserole

2 1/2 cups cooked chicken, diced or 2 (10 oz.) cans of chunk chicken

1 lb. tater tots

1/2 cup celery, chopped fine

1 (10.5 oz.) can cream of mushroom soup

1/2 cup mayonnaise

Preheat oven to 350 degrees F.

In a large bowl, combine chicken, celery, soup and mayonnaise. Layer 1/2 of the tater tots in the bottom of a well-greased 1-1/2 qt. casserole dish. Pour in chicken mixture and top with remaining tater tots. Bake uncovered for 1 hour at 350 degrees F.

Yield: 4 servings.

Fettuccine Alfredo

10 oz. fettuccine

1 oz. butter

8 oz. half-and-half

1/4 cup grated Parmesan cheese

Cracked black pepper

Bring a large pot of salted water to a boil. Cook pasta until 3/4 cooked. Strain off water and return pasta to the pot. Add butter and half-and-half. Bring to a hard boil.

When pasta is fully cooked, remove from the heat. Add black pepper and cheese. Toss and serve.

Yield: 2 servings.

Baked Beans

2 (1 lb. each) cans pork & beans

3/4 cup brown sugar, packed

1 teaspoon dry mustard

6 slices crispy bacon, crumbled

1/2 cup ketchup

Preheat oven to 350 degrees F.

In a small bowl, combine brown sugar and mustard. Place 1 can of beans in a large casserole dish. Sprinkle 1/2 of the brown sugar mixture over beans. Pour in second can of beans. Sprinkle bacon pieces on top and pour ketchup over that. Sprinkle remaining brown sugar and mustard mix on top.

Bake uncovered at 350 degrees F for 2 1/2 hours. Do not stir until finished.

Yield: 6 servings.

Baked Rice

2 tablespoons butter or margarine

1/2 cup onion, chopped

1 1/2 cups cooked rice

3 cups boiling water

1 teaspoon salt

1/4 cup parsley, chopped

1 cup cooked peas

Preheat oven to 350 degrees F.

Melt butter or margarine in large saucepan. Add onion and sauté 2 to 3 minutes. Add rice and stir until well coated with butter. Cook over low heat about 5 minutes. Add boiling water. Stir in salt.

Remove from heat and transfer to a large casserole dish. Cover tightly and bake at 350 degrees F for 25 minutes. Add parsley and warm peas. Fluff rice with a fork.

Yield: 4 servings.

Spinach with Garlic

1 1/2 lb. fresh spinach

2 teaspoons olive oil

1 head garlic, separated into cloves, peeled, and chopped

Salt to taste

Wash the spinach well, drain, and remove large stems. If leaves are very large, cut them in half; otherwise leave them whole. Heat the olive oil in a large, heavy skillet and add the garlic. Sauté, stirring for 2 minutes.

Add the spinach in batches as it wilts down, and pour off any liquid that accumulates. Sauté just until all the spinach is wilted and bright green. Add salt. Serve as is or season with one of the following: fresh lemon juice, balsamic vinegar, or red-pepper flakes.

Yield: 3 servings.

Squash Peach Bake

2 1/2 cups sliced unpeeled zucchini or yellow crookneck squash

Salt

1 cup sliced fresh peaches

2 tablespoons brown sugar, packed

2 1/2 tablespoons butter or margarine

Preheat oven to 350 degrees F.

Salt squash lightly. In a greased 2-quart baking dish, arrange squash and peaches in alternate layers. Sprinkle top with brown sugar; dot with butter. Cover and bake at 350 degrees F for 45 minutes or until squash is tender.

Yield: 4 servings.

Easy No-Boil Macaroni and Cheese

2 cups uncooked elbow macaroni

1 (12 oz.) container small curd cottage cheese

1 lb. shredded Cheddar cheese

Water to cover

4 tablespoons butter

Preheat oven to 350 degrees F.

Spray a 2-quart baking dish with non-stick cooking spray. Combine macaroni, cottage cheese and cheese in a large bowl. Pour macaroni mixture into prepared baking dish.

Add just enough water to the dish to cover noodles and cheese. Dot with butter. Bake at 350 degrees F for one hour or until macaroni is tender and cheese is melted.

Yield: 6 to 8 servings.

Elegant Green Beans

3 slices bacon

1 (16 oz.) can green beans

1 (3 oz.) package cream cheese, softened

1 tablespoon milk

1/2 teaspoon dried dill weed

Cook bacon in a medium skillet until crisp. Drain; reserve drippings in skillet. Crumble bacon and set aside. Drain green beans; reserve 1/4 cup liquid. Add reserved green bean liquid and green beans to drippings in skillet. Cook until heated through.

In a small bowl, mix crumbled bacon, cream cheese, milk and dill weed. Stir until no cream cheese lumps remain. Spoon over green beans.

Yield: 3 servings.

Corn Casserole

5 oz. very fine noodles

1/4 lb. American cheese, cubed

1/2 cup butter or margarine

1/3 cup sugar

1 (15.25 oz.) can cream-style corn

Salt and pepper, to taste

Preheat oven to 350 degrees F.

Cook noodles as directed on package. In a large bowl, combine all ingredients. Pour into a greased 1 1/2-quart casserole. Bake at 350 degrees F for 30 to 40 minutes.

Yield: 4 servings.

Rice Casserole

1 cup uncooked rice

1/2 lb. mushrooms

1/2 cup butter

1 (10.5 oz.) can French onion soup

1 (14.5 oz.) can beef bouillon

Preheat oven to 400 degrees F.

In a large saucepan, sauté rice and mushrooms in butter. Add onion soup and bouillon. Pour into greased 2-quart casserole dish. Bake at 400 degrees F for 1 hour.

Yield: 4 servings.

Veggie Casserole

1 (10 oz.) package frozen cauliflower

1 (10 oz.) package frozen broccoli

1 (10.5 oz.) can cream of mushroom soup

1 (8 oz.) jar processed cheese spread

1 (6 oz.) can French-fried onions

Preheat oven to 350 degrees F.

Spray a 2-quart casserole dish with non-stick cooking spray. Line dish with frozen vegetables. Spread mushroom soup over vegetables. Spread cheese over soup.

Bake at 350 degrees F for 35 minutes and then mix well. Sprinkle one can of French-fried onions over top and return to oven for 10 to 15 minutes.

Yield: 6 to 8 servings.

Squash Casserole

1 cup cooked yellow squash, mashed

1 cup cracker crumbs

1 cup milk

1 cup grated cheddar cheese

2 eggs

Preheat oven to 300 degrees F.

In a large bowl, combine all ingredients; bake in a 2-quart casserole dish in at 300 degrees F for 1 hour.

Yield: 2 servings.

Baked Beans

2 (15 1/2 oz.) cans pork and beans (drain 1 can)

2 tablespoons La Choy brown gravy sauce

1/4 cup brown sugar

2 tablespoons bacon bits

Preheat oven to 200 degrees F.

In a large bowl, combine all ingredients, making sure brown sugar is dissolved. Pour into a 2-quart baking dish; bake at 200 degrees F for 2 hours, stirring after 1 hour.

Yield: 6 servings.

Celery and Water Chestnuts

5 heaping cups celery, sliced diagonally, and leaves

1 (10.5 oz.) can cream of chicken soup

1 (6 oz.) can water chestnuts, drained and sliced

1 (4 oz.) jar chopped pimento

1 (2 oz.) pkg. slivered almonds

Preheat oven to 350 degrees F.

In a medium saucepan, cook celery, covered, for 5 minutes in a small amount of water. Drain. Combine with soup, water chestnuts and pimento.

Place in a 1 1/2-qt. baking dish and bake for 30 minutes at 350 degrees F. Top with slivered almonds.

Yield: 6 servings.

Cookies, Bars

& Candies

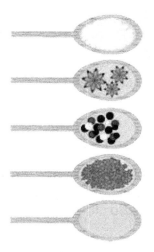

Black Walnut Cookies

2 cups brown sugar, packed

4 eggs, beaten

1/2 cup flour

1/2 teaspoon baking powder

1/2 teaspoon salt

4 cups black walnuts, chopped

Preheat oven to 375 degrees F.

In a medium bowl, beat sugar and eggs together until well mixed. In a large bowl, mix together flour, baking powder and salt, gradually add to the egg mixture. Stir in the walnuts.

Drop by spoonfuls onto a cookie sheet sprayed with non-stick cooking spray or use parchment paper. Bake at 375 degrees F for 10 to 12 minutes.

Yield: 5 dozen cookies.

Tiny Peanut Butter Balls

1 1/2 cups peanut butter

1/2 cup butter

1 teaspoon vanilla

2 2/3 cups confectioners' sugar

1 (20 to 24 oz.) package chocolate almond bark

In a large bowl, combine peanut butter, butter, vanilla and confectioners' sugar. Roll dough into tiny balls. Melt the almond bark in microwave, stirring every 30 seconds until melted. Put 1 drop of melted chocolate in tiny paper cups. Put 1 ball of peanut butter mixture over chocolate. Put 1 drop of chocolate on top.

Yield: 100 to 150 balls.

Reese Peanut Butter Squares

1 cup butter

1 1/2 cups crushed graham crackers

1 cup chunky peanut butter

2 1/2 cups confectioner's sugar

1 (12 oz.) chocolate bar

In a saucepan, melt butter. Remove from heat and add graham cracker crumbs. Add peanut butter and sugar and blend together thoroughly. Press into greased 13x9x2-inch baking dish. Melt chocolate in microwave. Spread chocolate over top. Place in refrigerator until hard. Heat knife to cut into squares.

Yield: 20 to 30 squares.

Butter Cookies

1 cup margarine or butter

1/2 cup brown sugar, packed

2 egg yolks

2 cups flour

1 teaspoon vanilla

Preheat oven to 400 degrees F.

In a large bowl, cream margarine or butter and brown sugar together. Add egg yolks, then flour and vanilla; mix well. Drop by rounded teaspoonfuls on cookie sheets, one inch apart. Bake at 400 degrees F for 10 to 12 minutes.

Yield: 1 to 2 dozen cookies.

Walnut Lace Cookies

1/2 cup butter or margarine

1/2 cup light corn syrup

2/3 cup brown sugar, packed

1 cup flour

1 cup walnuts, finely chopped

Preheat oven to 350 degrees F.

Melt butter or margarine in saucepan. Add corn syrup and brown sugar, and bring to a boil; remove from heat. Stir flour and nuts into the mixture. Drop by teaspoonfuls on cookie sheets. Bake at 350 degrees F for 8 to 10 minutes.

Yield: 6 dozen cookies.

Raisin Drops

1 cup butter or margarine

1 cup sugar

2 eggs

2 cups flour

1 cup raisins, soaked for 1 hour in 1/2 cup rum

Preheat oven to 400 degrees F.

In a large bowl, cream butter or margarine and sugar. Add eggs and beat well. Stir in well-drained raisins and flour. Drop by rounded teaspoonfuls onto cookie sheet, about two inches apart. Bake at 400 degrees F for 8 to 10 minutes until edges are lightly browned.

Yield: 6 dozen cookies.

Granola Bars

2 cups granola cereal with raisins

1/4 cup brown sugar, packed

1/4 cup sunflower kernels

1 large egg, lightly beaten

1 teaspoon vanilla extract

Preheat oven to 350 degrees F.

In a large bowl, combine all ingredients. Press evenly into a well-greased 8-inch square baking dish. Bake at 350 degrees F for 18 to 20 minutes. Cool in baking dish on a wire rack 5 minutes and cut into bars. Store in an airtight container.

Yield: 1 dozen.

No-Bake Peanut Butter Bars

2 cups graham crackers, crushed

1 cup butter, melted

1 cup peanut butter

3 1/2 cups confectioners' sugar

1 cup chocolate chips

In a large bowl, combine graham crackers, butter, peanut butter and confectioners' sugar until creamy. Press into a 13x9x2-inch baking dish. Melt chocolate chips in microwave, stirring at 30 seconds intervals. Frost with melted chocolate chips. Refrigerate to set the chocolate and cut into bars.

Yield: 2 dozen bars.

Chocolate Mint Snowballs

2 cups whipping cream, whipped

1 (16 oz.) package miniature marshmallows

1/2 cup crushed peppermint candy

1/2 cup pecans, chopped

1 (9 oz.) package chocolate wafers, crushed

In a bowl, combine the whipped cream, marshmallows, candy and pecans. Cover and refrigerate for 3 hours or overnight.

Stir marshmallow mixture; shape by 1/2 cupfuls into balls. Place chocolate wafer crumbs on a plate; roll marshmallow mixture in crumbs until coated. Keep refrigerated.

Yield: 20 servings.

Easy Peanut Butter Cookies

1 cup sugar

1 egg

1 cup peanut butter

1 teaspoon vanilla extract

Preheat oven to 350 degrees F.

In a large bowl, combine sugar, egg, peanut butter and vanilla; mix well. Spray a cookie sheet with non-stick cooking spray. Shape batter by tablespoonfuls into balls; place 2 inches apart on a cookie sheet. Flatten to 1/4 inch thickness by pressing with a fork in a crisscross design.

Bake at 350 degrees F for 10 minutes or until golden brown. Cool on cookie sheet for 1 minute. Remove to wire rack to cool completely.

Yield: 1 to 1 1/2 dozen.

No Bake Bon Bons

1 cup peanut butter

1 cup honey (mild)

1/2 cup carob powder

2 cups rolled oats

3/4 cup chopped nuts or coconut

In a large bowl, blend peanut butter and honey together until smooth, add carob and rolled oats until all is coated. Roll into 1-inch balls and finish by rolling in finely chopped nuts or coconut whichever you prefer. Store in airtight container.

Yield: 24 servings.

Wheat Sticks

2 cups whole-wheat flour

2 cups white flour

3/4 cup shortening

1 teaspoon salt

1/2 cup sugar

1 cup water

Preheat oven to 325 degrees F.

In a large bowl, combine flours, salt and sugar; cut in shortening with a pastry cutter or two knives until mixture is size of small peas. Add water. Knead and press into a cookie sheet. Cut into strips before baking. Bake at 325 degrees for about 45 minutes.

Yield: 45 servings.

Honey Popcorn Balls

3/4 cup sugar

1 tablespoon corn syrup

1/2 cup water

3/4 cup honey

3 qt. freshly popped corn, salted

16 all day suckers

In a medium saucepan, combine sugar, corn syrup and water. Cook to brittle stage. Add honey; cool 1 minute longer. Dribble hot liquid over the popcorn and shape around the suckers, leaving the handles out. Dipping your hands in cold water makes shaping easier.

Yield: 16 servings.

Perfect Chocolate Cookies

2 tablespoons butter

1 1/2 cups of chocolate chips

1 cup flour

1 (14 oz.) can sweetened condensed milk

1 cup pecans

Preheat oven to 325 degrees F.

Melt butter and chocolate chips in microwave in a medium bowl. In a large bowl, mix flour, sweetened condensed milk and pecans. Add butter and chocolate chip mixture.

Spray a cookie sheet with non-stick cooking spray. Drop on cookie sheet and flatten a little. Bake exactly 10 minutes at 325 degrees F.

Yield: 2 dozen cookies.

Swedish Cookies

1 cup butter

1/2 cup confectioners' sugar

1 3/4 cups flour

1 cup pecans, chopped

1 teaspoon vanilla

Preheat oven to 350 degrees F.

In a large bowl, cream butter. Add sugar slowly. Add flour, nuts and vanilla. Refrigerate. Roll in small balls and pat down to size on cookie sheet. Bake about 12 minutes at 350 degrees F. When done, roll in confectioners' sugar.

Yield: 1 1/2 dozen cookies.

Chocolate Truffles with Chocolate Crème Centers

Tip: Leave most of the candies in the refrigerator or freezer when doing the final step of coating with chocolate.

1 cup whipping cream
10 oz. semi-sweet chocolate chips
3 tablespoons butter
1 1/4 cups coarsely chopped toasted unblanched almonds
2 (12 oz.) bags semi-sweet chocolate chips or large chocolate bars equivalent to 24 oz. (for covering candy)

In a medium saucepan, heat cream to simmering on medium to medium high heat. Heat until it just starts to boil. Remove from heat. Add chocolate chips and butter. Whisk until smooth. Cool to lukewarm. Stir in almonds. Pour into a large bowl and refrigerate covered, stirring occasionally for 4 hours or overnight.

Using a spoon, scrape dough across the top and roll into 1" balls. Freeze on baking sheet until hard.

In a medium saucepan, melt 24 oz. chocolate chips or large chocolate bars over hot water (not boiling). Dip candy in chocolate using spoon or toothpicks. Line a baking sheet with wax paper. Put candy on baking sheet and freeze or refrigerate until hard. Yield: 4 1/2 dozen.

Tiger Butter

1 lb. almond bark, broken into pieces

1/2 cup chunky peanut butter

1/2 cup semi-sweet chocolate chips

4 teaspoons half and half

In a medium bowl, heat almond bark and peanut butter on MEDIUM in microwave for 3 to 4 minutes or until melted. Mix well and pour onto foil lined baking sheet that has been sprayed with non-stick cooking spray. Spread into a thin layer.

In a medium bowl, heat chocolate chips and half and half on HIGH in microwave 30 seconds or until chips are soft. Stir until smooth and then pour and swirl over almond bark mixture. Drag knife through mixture to create more swirls. Freeze for 5 minutes and then break into pieces.

Yield: 40 candies.

Chocolate-Peanut Butter Pile-Up

1 cup peanut butter

1 egg

1/2 cup sugar

1 (4 oz.) pkg. baking sweet chocolate, broken in pieces or 1 small pkg. chocolate chips

Preheat oven to 325 degrees F.

In a medium bowl, combine peanut butter, egg and sugar. Press or roll dough into a 10 x 7-inch rectangle on an ungreased baking sheet. Bake at 325 degrees for 20 minutes. Remove from oven. Immediately sprinkle chocolate on top and cover lightly with aluminum foil. Let it stand 2 or 3 minutes; remove foil. Spread chocolate over entire surface and immediately cut into 2 x 1-inch bars. Cool.

Yield: 30 candies.

Macaroons

2 egg whites

1 cup coconut

2 cups corn flakes

1 cup sugar

1 teaspoon vanilla

Preheat oven to 350 degrees F.

In a large bowl, beat egg whites until stiff; slowly add sugar, beating constantly. Fold in vanilla, corn flakes and coconut. Drop by teaspoonfuls on cookie sheets. Bake at 350 degrees F for 15 minutes.

Yield: 2 dozen cookies.

Special K Cereal Cookies

1 cup white corn syrup

1 cup granulated sugar

1 1/2 cups peanut butter

5 cups Special K cereal

Melt corn syrup and sugar together in saucepan over low heat. Stir in peanut butter and mix, then add cereal and gently mix just until all is coated. Drop on waxed paper and place in refrigerator to set.

Yield: 3 dozen.

Easy Chocolate Fudge

1 (12 oz.) package chocolate chips

1 (14 oz.) can sweetened condensed milk

1 teaspoon vanilla

1 1/4 cups walnuts, chopped (opt.)

Combine chocolate chips and milk in a microwaveable bowl and microwave on HIGH for 3 minutes; stir until smooth. Stir in vanilla and nuts. Using an 8-inch foil lined baking dish, pour fudge and spread evenly. Refrigerate until firm, about 2 hours.

Yield: 20 candies.

Praline Cookies

9 graham crackers (one package of a 14.4 oz. box)

1/2 cup margarine

1/2 cup butter

1/2 cup sugar

3/4 cup pecans, chopped

Preheat oven to 350 degrees F.

Break crackers into rectangles. Lay close together on baking sheets. In a medium saucepan, boil margarine, butter and sugar for 2 minutes. Pour over crackers. Sprinkle nuts over top.

Bake for 8 minutes at 350 degrees F. Remove from pan while hot and place on waxed paper.

Yield: 2 dozen cookies.

Almond Bark Cookies

1/2 (20 to 24 oz.) package almond bark

2 cups stick pretzels, broken

2 cups crisp rice cereal

1 or 2 cups dry roasted peanuts

Melt almond bark in microwave in a microwave-safe dish. Transfer to a large bowl and add pretzels, crisp rice cereal and peanuts; mix well. Drop on wax paper to cool.

Yield: 2 dozen cookies.

Country Sugar Cookies

1/2 cup butter

1 cup sugar

1 egg

2 cups flour

1/2 teaspoon vanilla

Preheat oven to 375 degrees F.

In a large bowl, cream together butter and sugar. Blend in egg. Add flour. Blend vanilla into mixture. Bake on cookie sheet at 375 degrees F for 10 to 12 minutes.

Optional - Glaze cookies with 3/4 cup powdered sugar mixed with 3 to 4 teaspoons water. Glaze and decorate cookies while still warm.

Yield: 2 dozen cookies.

Cakes, Pies

& Desserts

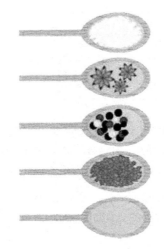

Key Lime Pie

1 (14 oz.) can condensed sweetened milk

3 whole eggs, separated

1 additional egg white

1/3 cup fresh key lime juice

2 pie crusts

Preheat oven to 300 degrees F.

In a large bowl, blend condensed milk, and the yolks of the 3 eggs. Beat for 2 minutes. Add the key lime juice and beat well. In a separate bowl, beat the 4 egg whites until stiff and dry and fold into the milk mixture.

Pour into pie crusts and bake at 300 degrees F for 10 minutes or until set. Cool thoroughly and top with refrigerated whipped topping, if desired. Refrigerate for several hours.

Apple Crisp

4 to 6 medium tart apples

1 1/2 cups oatmeal

1 1/2 cups brown sugar

2/3 cup flour

2/3 cup butter

Preheat oven to 350 degrees F.

Slice apples and spread on bottom of 13x9x2-inch baking dish. Sprinkle with cinnamon. Combine oatmeal, brown sugar, flour and butter ingredients. Crumble over apples. Sprinkle with more cinnamon. Bake at 350 degrees F 35 to 40 minutes or until apples are tender.

Yield: 4 to 6 servings.

German Chocolate Caramel Cake

1 (18 oz.) package German chocolate cake mix

1 (14 oz.) can sweetened condensed milk

1 (12.25 oz.) jar caramel ice cream topping

1 (8 oz.) container whipped topping

1/4 cup pecans, chopped

In a 13x9x2-inch baking dish, bake cake mix according to package directions. While cake is still warm from the oven, make holes 1 to 2 inches apart all over cake, using handle of wooden spoon. Pour the sweetened condensed milk over surface of cake.

Spoon the caramel topping on top and spread evenly on cake. When cake is completely cooled, top with whipped topping and sprinkle with chopped nuts.

Yield: 30 servings.

Cowboy Coffee Cake

2 (11 oz.) cans refrigerated buttermilk biscuits

1/4 cup butter or margarine, melted

1/3 cup brown sugar, packed

1/3 cup pecans, chopped

1 teaspoon ground cinnamon

Preheat oven to 350 degrees F.

Arrange biscuits in a lightly greased 9-inch round cake pan, overlapping edges. In a small bowl, combine butter or margarine, brown sugar, pecans and cinnamon; spread evenly over biscuits. Bake at 350 degrees F for 22 minutes or until golden. Serve warm.

Yield: 1 9-inch coffee cake.

Chocolate Almond Velvet

1 (16 oz.) can chocolate syrup

1 (14 oz.) can sweetened condensed milk

2 pints whipping cream

2 teaspoons vanilla extract

1/2 cup slivered almonds, toasted

In a mixing bowl, combine chocolate syrup, condensed milk, whipping cream and vanilla; beat until stiff peaks form. Fold in almonds. Spread into an ungreased 13x9x2-inch baking dish. Cover and freeze for 4 hours or until firm. Remove from freezer 5 minutes before serving.

Yield: 16 to 20 servings.

No Bake Pumpkin Pie

2 cups milk

2 (3/4 oz. each) boxes instant vanilla pudding

1 cup pumpkin

1 cup refrigerated whipped topping

1 teaspoon pumpkin pie spice

In a large bowl, combine all ingredients; pour into a graham cracker pie crust. Refrigerate 3 hours before serving.

Never Fail Pie Crust

2 cups flour

1/8 teaspoon salt

1 cup vegetable oil

1 egg

1 teaspoon vinegar

In a large bowl, mix flour, salt and oil until the size of peas. Combine egg and vinegar in a measuring cup and fill to 1/2 cup with cold water. Add to flour and mix well. Shape into a ball and chill for 1 hour. Roll out on floured surface to fit 2 9" pie plates.

Yield: two 9-inch pie crusts.

Free Recipe Cards

Just print the recipe cards and fill out.

Or copy the recipe card into Microsoft Word

and type your recipe.

InJars.com/recipe-cards.html

Other Books by Bonnie Scott

IN JARS SERIES – InJars.com

100 Easy Recipes in Jars
100 More Easy Recipes in Jars
Desserts in Jars

CAMPING – CampingFreebies.com

100 Easy Camping Recipes
Camping Recipes: Foil Packet Cooking

Bacon Cookbook: 150 Easy Bacon Recipes
Slow Cooker Comfort Foods
150 Easy Classic Chicken Recipes
Grill It! 125 Easy Recipes
Soups, Sandwiches and Wraps
Simply Fleece
4 Ingredient Cookbook
Fish & Game Cookbook
Cookie Indulgence: 150 Easy Cookie Recipes
Pies and Mini Pies
Holiday Recipes: 150 Easy Recipes and Gifts

CPSIA information can be obtained
at www.ICGtesting.com
Printed in the USA
FSOW04n1912151216
28615FS